Life
UNUSUAL

Winifred Mena Ajakpovi

ISBN: 978-978-985-368-7

Cover design: BramoDigi

Published by:
Heart2World Publishing
info@heart2worldpublishing.org
30, Muyiwa Opaleye street. Surulere

For information on distributions, translations, or bulk sales,
please contact
Winifred Mena Ajakpovi
winifredmena@gmail.com

Dedication

To everyone who desires a life filled with wonders, purpose, and fulfilment.

REVIEWS ON LIFE UNUSUAL

It is not very often that a writer can capture the journey of her life in a way that resonates with the reader while also highlighting the uniqueness of her personal experiences. This book has succeeded in doing that very well. No matter your place in life, this book will encourage, challenge, inspire and empower you. The many ebbs and flows of the writer's unusual life will embolden you to be fearless in the journey of life, while subtly but yet convincingly compelling you to believe that the time tested principles of God and humanity should never be compromised as you do so.

It is a must-read for any young girl questioning her self worth or purpose, and for the grown woman who has lost all hope that the dreams she nursed as a little girl are all but lost.

Claudia N Oboniye
LL.B., B.L., LL.M., PH.D Candidate (UBC); Principal, Ejogian Law Group (Chicago, Canada); Foreign Legal Consultant, DCK Solicitors (London, UK), Deaconess, RGGC, USA

The LIFE UNUSUAL book is a must read, full of the Writer's very unique experiences and insights, and written for everyone who desires more than the ordinary life! The Writer inspires, builds faith & sparks creativity and boldness in the reader.

Ihuoma Azuike MPH
Project Manager II
CHI St Luke's Health
Houston, Texas
USA

Life Unusual is unlike any other career book you have read! It's riveting, compelling and born out of a genuine desire to inspire us with one of the most effective yet unusual approaches to a successful career path. Each chapter ends with some valuable reflections that prepare us for our daily challenges.

A must read for all!!

Dorothy Chimezie
Educator, Houston independent School District. Houston TX

It's been a long time I read a book containing 14 chapters which left me eager to read more chapters!

'Life Unusual' makes for an excellent reading, it is an insightful compilation of 'unusual revelations' in the author's career and life journey.

CONTENT

With this book, the Writer has simply demystified "Career Planning" and made it appealing through captivating stories filled with life lessons. The candour and eloquence of her storytelling is unbeatable and I simply love chapter 6 where the story telling meets with action planning through the Career tool kit she provided. She made it simple to figure out what intervention you need to embrace to unlock your potential.

Though not majorly a Christian book, I cannot but describe this beautiful book as faith based because the author zooms in on the God factor in her story telling. Chapter 9 is fully dedicated to show casing the power of God in her life journey and as a close witness in her life journey, I cannot but applaud the excellence in her recollection of God's almightiness.

I am confident to recommend this book to early career starters and mid-career persons who may be faced with challenging situations.

'Life Unusual' is a sure Companion for Career Success.

Funke Amobi
Country Head, HR
STANBICIBTC BANK

This book is a compelling read for anyone starting a career journey providing insights and nuggets required to succeed while being anchored on God.

Yinka Adelekan
MD Agustin and Co
Nigeria

We can all agree that 2020 has been the most unusual of years. There seems to be no better time than now to be blessed with Winifred's book, LIFE UNUSUAL.

Winifred takes us through a journey, navigating various facets of life, the challenges and the expectations, and how to be on top of each phase. I'm also honored to have watched her go through some of these phases and saw how much of a go-getter she was, and still is today.

As a mentor to many and someone who has lost a lot and gained so much within the past year, I am immensely grateful for this book and how it can help others navigate the highs and lows of life.

I can't wait to see the many lives that will be transformed by this book. Everyone needs to get one.

Ife Durosinmi- Etti
Founder, AGS Tribe

A few years ago, I began having serious conversations with myself about writing a book. I had traveled through the mountains and valleys of different fields working in roles from my legal profession, to banking to Human Resources - a place I fitted into like a round peg in a round hole.

The more I contemplated writing, the more it appeared it eluded me. Though the urge was there, I couldn't quite articulate what exactly my heart was saying.

Would it be about the many lessons and unforgettable memories from growing up in a family of 6 with 5 of us being girls and 1 brother?

Would it be about my work with youths in my hometown as I inspired and created a pathway for their growth and success?

Would it be about finding purpose? My passion so strong it easily competes with my job/career?

Would it be about my transition through many career paths and rising in the same?

OR, would it be about the miraculous turn of events in my journey where I did not have to sniff and scurry around to find the best jobs, but they came looking for me anyway?

I didn't quite know. I dropped the idea...only for it to return, haunting me down. I now believe that authors do not choose the book to write, books choose their authors. This book had to be written by all means - and it chose me.

It's my story.

This is a memoir chronicling critical events in my life that shaped me into the woman I am - and still becoming.

In many ways, it will serve as a handbook for career professionals for men and women desiring to rise through the ranks in their industry. It will also serve as an inspiration to someone trying to find purpose and birth same.

It's a compilation of principles, values, and the ethics you need to stand out in your field and make yourself the obvious choice like my dear boss turned sister would often say.

In this book, I want to make you my friend, my conversation buddy, and sibling as we go along. It is not just another book; consider this a treasure chest and I'm willing to share it with you.

Each chapter comes with key lessons for your own journey.

Winifred Mena Ajakpovi
2020

CHAPTER ONE

In the  BEGINNING *Begin*

This thing we call life is not a destination with an end but a path down which we continue to journey as long as we can breathe. Life is to be lived not squandered or to give away waiting for the end to close upon us.

- Byron Pulsifer

I s the future certain or is it what we make of it? I believe it's both. It is sure to end in some good place - or at least we expect it to be great. There are times of uncertainty that are inevitable in our life's journey.

The moments when one phase of life comes to an end and a transition is needed, is often the most delicate moments in the journey of life.

As a young lawyer coming out of National Youth Service, I wondered what the future held.

On one hand, I believed and hoped for the best and on other hand, I felt so pressured due to a subtle innate feeling of desiring to make a point with my life, to maintain the track record of success and most importantly, to live up to - if not beat - the expectations that I was convinced others had of me.

In the company of 4 of my friends, we returned from the eastern part of the country to the capital, the bright lights, hungry, charged up and ready to seize the opportunities that the city had to offer us.

After all, we had obeyed the clarion call and completed the mandatory one year national youth service every young school leaver was required to complete. Now we expected the land to serve us well, with great jobs. We were young, bold, fierce, sassy, smart and ready to take on the world.

I had it all figured out, the kind of job that would be-fit me. But it was not quite as easy as I had imagined, and the dots were not connecting as quickly too.

Our job hunting spree continued for about 4 months and then one after the other, my friends began to get jobs and we were overly excited by the turn of events. My own news of, "Hey girls, I just got a job" was around the corner, I believed. But then, our new life of submitting CVs and scanning the landscape for opportunities was temporarily halted due to the news that hit us right between the chests.

Towards the end of that year, my best friends (we were a gang of 5) had traveled for the Christmas holidays While 3 made it home safely, Nthabi our curvy, pretty fun-to-be-with diva friend and Florence, gave us something to cry about. A fatal accident terminated not only their journey, but their lives too.

This was a particularly painful and troubling moment for us as friends and a defining one as we had grown from friends to sisters, sharing a special bond across several years. Anyway, burials done, lessons learnt, pain absorbed, and life continued, job hunting continued.

So I lived with an aunt and soon enough, I had to seek a new home. Thank you aunty, those days added to my quest for success in a city where I had no one, on my own with nothing but God and my boldness and quite frankly, my conviction that there wasn't any other way but success!. I knew it as certain as the sun would rise.

With the upbringing, family background, and qualifications I had, I totally believed finding my dreams would be a walk in the park.

Watch out world, I'm here!

But life had a lot to teach me I soon found out.

It was a shock to me when months passed and I was still on the long wait list for that opportunity, all my friends were on their way to accomplishing our early life's goals, what was going on? My first lesson in patience!

I learnt very quickly that when life serves you lemons you quickly make lemonades. You will realize too that this is not a cliché, the day you walk similar path. So despite the fact that my dream job having eluded me, I secured a job in a Law Firm, the next best thing. It wasn't a particularly large one or one of the dream places I desired to work in but I celebrated it. In many ways, that firm taught me and trained me for the bigger picture I had in mind.

Remember my tribe of sisters? My 4 precious sisters? They were like angels during this period. I have a brother in the mix too, but he is the baby of the house. Together we were all inseparable even till date.

So, even when my job was not so fantastic, my sister Barbie (God bless her soul) made sure she doubled my pay. For every dime I earned in that Law firm she topped it with an equal dime. This kept me at par with my friends which was very important to me at the time, living up to external expectations.

A lesson I later learnt that I only had myself as competition to beat my last performance each time, not anyone else's standards or expectations.

Talking about one's journey evokes various kinds of feelings and a few tears too. It opens you up to yourself in a new way and you become, through imagination, a spectator in your own journey, reliving events, conversations and memories that are unforgettable.

If I could travel through the loins of time to meet with my younger self, I would pat Winifred on the back, hold her tightly in a warm embrace and say to her, "It's alright, Winifred. No pressures. No hurries. Keep putting in the work, those who need you are already waiting for you. You are awesome and would do just fine."

In the words of the co-founder of Apple, "Life really makes sense when we look back. It is then we can really connect the dots."

Key Lessons

☒ Life is truly a Teacher - maybe not the best, but it is a very good one. Reality often differs from the ideas we've painted in our heads about who we are, what we are capable of, and what we truly deserve.

☒ Staying level-headed and focused becomes increasingly difficult when attention is given to what others are doing or whatever progress they are making. Watering your own garden is essential.

☒ Relationships are one of the strongest support systems you can ever have.

CHAPTER TWO

The CAREER EVOLUTION

THE CAREER EVOLUTION

"Our finest moments are most likely to occur when we are feeling deeply uncomfortable, unhappy, or unfulfilled. For it is only in such moments, propelled by our discomfort, that we are likely to step out of our ruts and start searching for different ways or truer answers."

- BM. Scott Peck

The manner in which I landed my first job, and then subsequent ones, made real to me the maxim that, "All that God would bring one's way will be channeled through men and women too. This taught me early in life to believe in "the gift of men".

A referral from my aunt to the Principal Partner in the Law firm I mentioned, terminated my relentless search to secure my first job. The man was friendly and amiable and we remain very good friends till date. He became a Father/Uncle figure to me on this journey as well.

Working in this Law Firm provided decent income, valuable experience, and more importantly, a place to deploy my skills.

I worked with this law firm for about a year before beating my path to a different career environment.

I was introduced to Mr. A.A as I would like to call him for the purpose of this book, an amazing, gentle and smart businessman. At that time, he was the CEO of a mortgage bank. By sheer providence, this man believed so much in me. He affirmed that I was smart, savvy, and up to the task. Without flinching, he offered me a middle management position as opposed to the entry level position I had expected.

I got into the role and my boss became my career mentor as his guidance was very instrumental to my growth. Permit me to remind you here of "the gift of men" I had come into the system as a green horn but in a short while, I grew in competence and capacity in many ways. I began early to build a network, a community of influencers.

I pulled in my weight and delivered promptly; excellence is as important as breathing is to me as a human. The thought of failing or not meeting up to demands is as far from me as the sky is from the earth. I never want to be associated with failure in any way.

As I write this, my first real boss and Mentor Mr. A. A, has passed on. He passed on years ago. When the news of his death came to me, it hit home. I felt it so deeply. I fondly remember him as a friend, mentor, and guide who contributed immensely to my growth. He took a bet on me despite not having deep knowledge of who Winifred was or is.

At the event of his demise, I promised myself to help anyone connected to him whenever the opportunity presented itself. This was my own little way of repaying his kind heart. Years later, I was able to fulfil that promise. This book, in some way, serves that purpose too. He gave me a head start - I'll be ever grateful.

The Mortgage bank was a very structured and formal organization. Working there equipped me in many ways. I was exposed to many new things as regards the professional world.

As much as this was beneficial to me, I occasionally took a peep at my colleagues who were working in bigger organizations at the time. Seeing them fly in their own path created an intense desire for me to reach for more.

Much as it was great to work here, I had my eyes on bigger things. While the Mortgage bank gave me some exposure, I still felt a bit of personal embarrassment and failure.

The next job came afterwards through another relationship, my Friend.

I got a job in a multi-national bank, a bigger organization. It was 40% owned by the French and 60% by Nigerians. My career took a quantum leap and there was no going back. I finally landed the job I felt befitted me.

My profile was now reading like I wanted it to, "This is it!" I must have thought to myself. Getting employed in the multinational organization was very close to what I had always desired. The bank was top of the charts in the banking world owing to how wealthy it was.

Despite how beautiful and great all of that was, the bank folded up due to many internal challenges - chief - which was mismanagement. Following the ill incident I secured another job in yet another bank. I had begun to toe the line of the financial services industry or so it seemed.

It was yet another great start but my hopes were to be dashed when this new bank folded up in the first week of my resumption, again!. Too short a journey it was that I had little to no experience to show for the time spent there.

I headed to work one fateful morning all dressed up and ready to seize my day at my new work place. You can only imagine my shock when I realized the entire premises was under lock and key. The bank had been sealed and no access into the premises was granted. My head fell in disappointment but I had to move on.

At this point, I felt there was a plot or a coup d'état planned by some unseen forces to sabotage my career growth.

It is definitely not a new phenomenon anywhere in the world, that financial institutions- and other types of institutions fold up. However, what was new to me was twice in a row? Something was either wrong with the economy or the financial services system or me. To be honest this did cross my mind a few times though confidence level made sure I didn't feel something was wrong with me or my choices, at least not for too long.

How was I to grow and gain mileage in my career by hopping from one job to another within a very short time?

I had my eyes on the big dream for my career, but the journey now seemed to be taking longer than I had ever imagined. The desire to seek another job waned with each attempt I made and I soon threw in the trowel.

Realizing my search yielded no result, I had to relocate to a different country for a while with the aim of resettling. While there, I engaged in a couple of jobs to keep myself together and distract myself from many things. Remember all this while life was happening and my peers and friends were all advancing in their careers. I learnt early that sometimes the way up is down!

What did you hear about idle hands? They are the devil's workshop, right? So, even if I wasn't at the exact career level that I had envisaged, my hands were kept busy and life was good. After sometime, I came back to Nigeria and resumed the job search. My search for a job consumed about another year before I finally secured one.

Another bank was my next point of call. It was a nice, funky, groovy bank at the time and a posh bank which made it very popular at the time. I was happy; I felt like I was again, coming back to where I belong.

From as far back as I could remember, I had a consciousness about my personal brand. I had always borne the notion that I had a personal brand to build and I was very conscious of it. This was even before I had built a network or achieved any level of growth. For this reason, I did not just seek after a better place to work but a reputable positioning.

Building my career Safety nest

Immediately I secured the new job in the new bank, I knew I had to do something different.

I couldn't agree more with the words of Vivian Jokotade - the Nigerian-American author and actress, who also said at a point in her journey, "I discovered that a fresh start is a process. A fresh start is a journey - a journey that requires a plan."

I needed a plan of action to birth the career success story I truly desired. It is only a mad man that keeps repeating the same action and hoping for a different result right? And I am certainly not mad. I needed a different type of action. I decided to try the God factor.

I wasn't the tongue-talking-demon-chasing-bible-thumping Christian at the time, but I had faith - even as small as a mustard seed - and that was enough to move my mountains.

Because this was my first job in a long time, my first pay cheque mattered a lot. Securing that first payment would have served as compensation for all the time expended seeking for a job. Rather than basking in the euphoria of finally getting paid a good sum after a long streak of challenges, I did something unusual. It was the only thing I thought I could do to secure my future. That was the beginning of my unusual career story.

I took my first pay cheque including all the other monetary benefits I received from the bank, then found my way to a church.

It wasn't a church I really knew or where I attended church regularly - it was just down the street. But I knew I could talk to God there.

When I informed my close friends about my plan to do this, they were shocked. They must have thought I had a night out with the fairies. But I went ahead, regardless.

Like a little girl appealing to the loving heart of her father, I poured out my heart before God. He had to hear me. The journey had not been particularly smooth or easy. The roller coaster rides of the many jobs I had, were now upsetting me so much I needed to get off that train.

I told God I was going to try Him at His word. He just had to come through for me. I told Him that I would give it all - my total pay cheque made up of all the annual benefits paid upfront and everything in between. This left me that period broke but I was rich in my heart! I gave everything and told God that I wanted to make a covenant with Him concerning my career.

Again, I did this, not necessarily being a great Christian but because the last two-three years had been rough and I didn't want to go through my career journey alone anymore so I sought out divine guidance.

After I said that prayer, I dropped the cheque for the entire sum into the offering basket not looking back.

If I could pour out the rhythms of my heart on that very day; I expressly told God, Thank you for this job, but I never want to look for a job again or have to apply for a job.

As I poured my heart out to God, memories of many jobs I applied for kept flashing through my mind. I had had my fair share of interviews, rejections, and even getting ridiculed or insulted at interview venues and I sure didn't want to have such experiences again so I told God that I never wanted to write an application letter again.

I also told God that if the company I was working in began having issues, He should take me out before it folds up or collapses. I said this prayer because it was a very turbulent time economically for the country and I unfortunately had been in too many companies that ran into troubled waters. I remember my friends teasing me and saying I was responsible for the downfall of all those companies and that anywhere I went ended up having issues leading up to a collapse. Kids are mean right?

And we were kids then. So yes, it was a joke at the time and we would all laugh over it but I guess I was discerning enough (at least about my brand if nothing else), to know I did not want that kind of joke around me. And so allow me to be philosophical, but this girl then, now woman, told God to "please, dear Lord, take me out of any company that is on a nosedive if ever, because I do not want to be ever associated with failure.

I walked out of that church that day with pockets empty and a heart full of faith. The favors, unexpected calls, and outturn of this singular act of faith ignited a string of experiences that are nothing but supernatural and today now make up my unusual career story. Lesson, there is no glory without pain.

Hitting the Iceberg

Like the famous Titanic that hit an iceberg deep in the middle of the Pacific, my little perfect bank met its end too. When I began to notice the shaking and challenges within the bank, I immediately, in my corner office, began to remind God of my Covenant with Him.

I needed to get on the next available lifeboat to set sail to the new place I was to continue my career journey. I would not sink with this boat or be termed a "boat-sinker" or "business crasher" again.

Key Lessons

- If there is anything my career journey has taught me, it is transitions. Movement is a proof of life and health. Being stuck or comfortable in one place is never advisable.

- It is that career or business is spiritual. Sorry if you don't share this truth but it is a truth and I believe it strongly. If you are in any of these areas, you better anchor your success on "something: and of which my recommendation is GOD.

- While at the beginning the many transitions and shaking I experienced were uncomfortable, the experience stretched me in critical areas of my life. I learned the power of focus. Like Dr. Martin Luther King roared that very day, I also had a dream and I kept at it.

- I learned persistence. I could count the rejections, insults, and "Nos" I received all through my search for a perfect landing for my career - in all, I kept pushing. I would not settle for less. One big YES cancels the several rejections and insults no matter how many they are.

Quirky Thoughts

The gift of men.

Thinking about one year I stuffed betrayal from three specific friends, it broke my heart.

That year (2012) I redefined the word "friend"

I then became more deliberate about who qualifies as a friend.

I learned to pray for and about the gift of friends, the gift of men. It is not to be taken lightly.

When God wants to bless, He uses men Because God is not going to come down from heaven and do stuff himself. He needs people.

May God give us the gift of men.

In all, I say thank you for the gift of special individuals like you.

And to my Father in Heaven, thank you for the gift of men in our lives.

Chapter Three

The only journey is the one within.

- Rainer Maria Rilke

*O**ur life is ever evolving*. I consider it similar to an encyclopedia with many different topics and broad knowledge areas. As we age, we discover the many interesting parts of our being; our talents, potentials, abilities. We also get to realize the dreams that keep us awake and tug at our hearts continually till we rise up to do something about them.

Discovering oneself is like opening a big book. Isn't it amazing that we use the word "destiny" to describe the outcome of our lives?

If that word were expanded, we can have DESTINATION. This "destination" is hinged on discovery.

Personal discovery is an internal journey everyone must undertake.

My own journey had four distinct phases.

The Discovery

I think I didn't know myself for quite a long time. As a child brought up in a loving and godly home with parents as models to follow, I was just the obedient child that followed every parental prompting and instructions.

When I reflect on the beautiful memories of growing up and my eventual career choices, I probably would have chosen an entirely different path.

Without a doubt, if I had the total freedom to express my inner passion, desires and dreams, I probably would have chosen Entertainment over Law.

I struggled with knowing who I really was. I always thought others had potentials, gifts, or abilities that I lacked.

As I made headway in my life, I realized that it was all my perspective - the lenses through which I viewed my world. I could change it. In a funny way, those whom I admired and thought had something I lacked, applauded me at every opportunity they had.

They'll say, "You're strong" "Winifred, you are good at what you do" "You bring excellence to the table, every time." I was just being 'myself,' yet they saw these as exceptional.

Does this sound like you in any way? If so you are in great company and I say welcome to life.

As a reserved person, I was usually the last to make friends in gatherings or where there were groups of people. Others did that pretty easily. I used to think I needed to change into becoming 'the life of the party' or the one who struck conversations quickly.

Before I realized my strength as a naturally quiet person and an observer, I thought I needed to be loud and friendly to make a head way in my career and I envied people who were loud and friendly.

Despite my personality, I forged ahead with speed in my career. I then realized that there was nothing wrong with being reserved and quiet after all. There is nothing weak about being reserved. I ditched the feeling of trying to be someone else and embraced the uniqueness of my personality.

Rather than wallowing in comparisons and an attempt to run away from ME, I chose to flourish in my space and with my natural strengths, I decided to be me.

I took a couple of personality tests and the more I did that, the more I found out about myself and the more I realized that there were people like me, which made me comfortable in my own skin and flaunting who I am.

Did I tell you, Dad was a lawyer and he worked for the government; same with my mum. We were and still are a very close family and we do everything possible together. Being all married now and settled, we all still meet up once a month, we holiday together, we exchange gifts and our husbands and wives have come to accept that that's the way the family is. There is no competition but rather a strong foundation of each one pull the other up.

I was always slightly different from my siblings though, a little crazy, a little snobbish, a little noisy, a little reserved, a little bold, a little quiet. Does that make sense to you? Winifred was a blend of it all. I remember specifically I was considered a spendthrift - I could dissipate any amount of money I was given and quickly too and ready for more.

My siblings on the other hand, somehow always had some money left over. Ask me how? I couldn't for the life of me fathom it. Like every parent will do, on one of those days, my parents decided to scold me and maybe talk some sense into their daughter.

"Why aren't you disciplined with your spending? What do you do with all the money we give you?"

My only response was, "I am going to make a lot of money and money will never be a problem to me. You don't have to worry about a thing!"

"The secret to living is giving."
- Tony Robbins.

Most of what has become my personal values today came out of watching my father live his own ideals. Though a Lawyer, he worked with the State Government in several capacities but always something around Human Resource management or personnel as it was then called, and leadership/governance. Principally, Dad was the go-to person for employment opportunities.

Our home soon became a meeting hub welcoming all kinds of people in need of one job opportunity or another. Dad was a shining light that others gravitated towards. In wonder, I watched as he, in his best way, attended to each one and helped them rise to a better place in their own lives.

He truly had a heart for people. So much did his life inspire me that on a day he took me to his office, I stopped him in his tracks and said, "Daddy, I'll like to do what you are doing when I grow up. I want to be able to help people just as you do."

At this point, I had caught his heart, his passion and his drive. I believe his examples, more than anything sharpened my understanding about myself and who I wanted to become. I have an incurable obsession to help people.

The Struggles

Being "unapologetically me" came with its own struggles too, but I'll pick this struggle over trying to be someone else.

My obsession to help people literally keeps me awake at night. As I grew in my career, I was obsessed with pulling other people up. Every single time a vacancy opened up in the companies I worked with, I created time to pray asking God to send my way, men and women who really needed the job.

On many occasions, I have received feedback from several employees affirming that all it took to get their job opportunity was their competence and the availability of the opportunity, nothing more. Each time I got that feedback, I smiled and I knew those were answered prayers. Having struggled with finding that leg in, that first opportunity, I was very passionate about careers and aiding people to come into their own. Winifred is that person who doesn't want to hurt people but desires the best for them.

Was this personality type of mine exploited? Definitely. Including some of the people reading this book. I then tried to be hard, tough and not care as much, but I just could not sustain that for a long time. It simply wasn't me.

I eventually had to find a balance between being tough and tender. Being friendly and firm can go together perfectly.

By my choice to play tough, I was attempting to live the life of another person who I am not. What a futile and unfulfilling adventure it was. If I could wear a cape now, it would have the words 'Be Unapologetically You' written boldly in spotted letters as I go about my daily life. Colleen Hoover was right, "You'll never be able to find yourself if you're lost in someone else."

Courage

I know beyond any doubt what my purpose is. I know I am called to make an impact. I live for people. I am a "people person" as they say. I won't definitely survive in a world where I am all alone - no matter the stupendous wealth and resources that will be available.

The all-important question of purpose must be answered in the journey of self-discovery. After all, purpose is the intent of a thing. Not understanding or living in it is a breeding ground for dissatisfaction and lack of fulfillment.

I am called to help. Helping people requires a measure of wealth, influence, and power. It is God's responsibility to place wealth in my hands and I have seen how He constantly puts resources at my disposal.

Acceptance

I can say that accepting who I am, was the biggest game changer for me, it brought the Midas Touch to everything I did. I have realized that some have their lives go in a linear progression where their dreams seem to fall in place as planned; others have to go round in circles. I consider every phase of my life instrumental to the next one.

Now that I've gained some considerable height in my career, the desire for the Entertainment Industry came hunting again. I decided this time to take a step in that direction regardless. I was bold enough to be me! Regardless. Regardless meant despite my strides in the corporate world, despite going to become a beginner in a new field (I have always known that sometimes the way up, can be down). Despite everyone's perception. This time I was ready to do it for ME.

It was not about peer pressure, it was not about the type of jobs my friends were getting or that I felt I should be doing, it was about what I wanted to do regardless.

So I got a part in my first movie, I left the office that day, later than I usually would, got into my car and drove out slowly. The ride was different and the route as well. This was what I had always wanted, my heart had desired this, since I was a little girl.

Now I had the chance, but the thoughts in my heart made the journey to the movie set even longer.

I kept thinking and questioning myself;

"What will people say?"
"What will my friends say?"
"Will the industry accept me?"

How quickly can I make a mark? I was in a hurry. Seems I am

always in a career hurry right? Self-inflicted pressure to succeed.

I had to shut down those thoughts and do it regardless.

Regardless of the struggles, failures and successes, it brought about a new revelation about who I was.

That's my journey. So, I ask you; when will you begin that long journey into yourself?

Key Lessons

- Having great models to follow has a compelling influence in shaping our perspectives about who we are and who we can become.

- Personal discovery is a life-long journey. You will get introduced to yourself many times as you come into new relationship networks, information and times spent in the secret place with God in prayer and devotion.

- True fulfillment comes from expressing the dreams that reside in your heart.

- And my personal all-time favorite is that there can be multiple expressions of one person. It is not possible that you were born to only do or be one thing and then die. No! Contemplate the story of the talents in the bible.

CHAPTER FOUR

The FRANTIC SEARCH

THE FRANTIC SEARCH

There are only two ways to live your life. One is as though nothing is a miracle. The other is as though everything is a miracle.

Albert Einstein

ife is unusual. We may be logical beings, but truly life is more than a product of logic. It is a miracle. Our life experiences should be filled with bursts of miracles and wonders as well. From the conception of a child in the womb, the fusion of cells and growth of bones, the crowning of the head of the baby in the process of childbirth, the mental and social evolution we go through to become change agents in society, they are all miraculous.

Taking a look at nature, it is a miracle. It calls for awe, wonder and unlimited discovery. How tender fickle plants can push through the hard and touch surface of the earth to emerge bearing precious seeds is nothing short of a miracle. Our lives should not be normal - by every sense of the word; it should be supernatural - unusual. Our lives should be an unusual expression of the amazing power and ability of God on the earth. My unusual career is a segment of my unusual life.

A life that desires to be unusual should not also do only usual things.

The fact that a process can be explained does not mean that is all there is to the story.

A lot of times people explain away miracles as some act of fate, coincidence or act of personal genius. In a world of self-made men and women, it may be hard to believe certain acts are largely supernatural.

When I think of acts that are life events yet miraculous, I imagine how Joseph felt when one night he slept in a dingy prison having been locked up for a crime he had no hand in, to wake up with a call from the most Powerful ruler of the time to solve an impending global hunger crisis. I imagine how Esther, an orphan, felt as she walked down the aisle to be presented to the King who eventually made her his Queen.

Our career journey can be filled with such miraculous feats too. Indeed, it should be. If we spend over 90000 hours of our earthly life working, it sure should be filled with bursts of miracles as well.

One fateful day, the head of the Human Resources (HR) department called and asked me into her office. This was not going to be another interview but she asked me almost immediately I stepped in, "Are you a Christian?" and I answered "Yes".

On the day I got the interview invite for this job, I put it off on account of my wedding plans and honeymoon immediately after, I was not available for any meetings that period of about 3 weeks... Even after I secured the job, I declined on account of pregnancy but an exception was made for me to resume, baby and all.

After I joined this organization, I didn't quite know who suggested my name or how my CV got into their hands. All my search to find out how the CV got there didn't yield result at first.

So, I continued working. The day I got the call from this company, I had just muttered a prayer to God regarding where I was. News had begun flying around as regards the bank I was in at the time having issues and being financially unstable to continue as a growing concern. I eventually made a switch to this new Bank where the Head of HR now called to ask me if I was a Christian.

Here is her story:

Where I worked like five years before I met Winifred Mena, it was a period of recruitment; and as usual, CVs were brought in and during the sorting process I found Winifred's CV, but for some reason she was not selected at this time. But, something about her name and her resume stood out for me. It registered for reasons I cannot yet tell.

When I moved to another organization, we also needed to hire new members of staff. As we went through the motions of finding the right fit, her name came up in my heart. I knew without a doubt that Winifred was the right fit for this role.

Where was I to begin the search? This was 5 years after seeing that CV and that was in another company where I worked.

I immediately drove to the company to see what I could find. The distance from where I lived to where the company was located was like two ends of a pole, but I went all the way, regardless.

On my arrival, I was informed that the Managing Director I knew while I worked with this particular organization had moved to another company. A member of staff directed me to write an application letter to the organization to request for that CV or to at least gain access to the pile of documents from that year.

Let me mention that all this did not take place in a day, it took a while.

I was then granted the permission to visit the warehouse of the company where unwanted documents were stored and after about four weeks of protocol, five bags of CVs were handed to me; five huge bags. I carried these bags home to begin my search.

Why would I want to go all this way to find one CV?

All the while, I could not completely remember the name, surname or anything to easily recognize that CV. I simply had an assurance in my heart that when I found the right one, I would certainly know.

Looking for her CV was as easy as seeking a needle in a haystack. For every time I wanted to give up, I had the nudge to keep on searching for the CV.

As dramatic as life can be, I didn't find this CV until the last bag.

As I sorted out one by one the CVs in the final sack, I found it. "Here you are!" I smiled congratulating myself for a job well done.

One way or the other, Winifred's CV registered in my heart so much so that 5 years after, I still could not get over it.

I believed this was divine and something spectacular was coming out of this.

Returning to the office, I dialed Winifred's number but she had changed it and was no longer reachable.

This was a dead-end, right?

After going through the toughest of steps to find this CV would I give up now?

Certainly not!

I dialed the last company she worked and they also informed me that she had moved to another company but by a stroke of luck, someone who knew her new organization volunteered the information.

Through him, I connected with Winifred – after five long years.

Connecting with Winifred proved that it was more than a work relationship we were to share. It was destiny. It was God trying to prove a point to her and to me.

Stories like these appear too good to be true. In a logical sense, this could be dismissed as fable to numb the mind from diligent hard work and pursuit to reliance on some "outside force" to get ahead in life. For some, it would stir them to ask for the favor of God to be active in their lives.

Looking at this another way, isn't our lives meant to be a script lived out? A script written by an amazing God who intends to demonstrate His ability even in the mundane details of our lives. The truth is, when it comes to God, if it appears too-good-to-be-true, then it probably is.

In her office that sunny afternoon within the walls of this beautiful organization, we broke down and tears welled up in our eyes as I saw how far God could move others to get His word to come to pass. It was more than I bargained for, far more than I could have imagined.

So, after the miracle of this job wore off, I moved again. Yes I changed jobs. Again another strange occurrence.

Again, I got a phone call to attend an interview for a job I never applied for in an organization I had searched but had not found my way into, God made a way. The day of the interview came and like the previous job, I couldn't attend again because this time I was down with the flu and had totally lost my voice. Innocently, I went to the organization to show myself and show how bad the situation was.

Strangely my interview was reduced to a few critical questions, I used part sign language and part words and part writings and that was it! God changes protocols for us. Did I get the job? What do you think? By now you should know its life unusual and career unusual for me. Yes I did, much to my surprise.

It was even more heart-rending and humbling to realize that I was the only external party interviewed for that role. 21 other members of staff within the organization who were equally qualified and in the know, were declined while I was offered the job without lifting a finger. As an HR Professional I know how difficult this can be, it had to be God.

Putting God first means God prioritizing every matter that relates to your life.

I have come to understand that work is more than "work" In other words, it isn't just to be a means of livelihood, or a place to receive a fat paycheck to fulfill your monthly goals.

There is purpose attached to it (as I would be sharing in the next chapter). At work, it isn't only bodies that connect - souls connect.

While still in this organization, one of the top Managers reached out to me and informed me of an opening - a higher position within this company that he felt I was qualified for. Here I was, working and being my best and being contented at it, yet opportunities came knocking on my door without me seeking them out.

If I could capture this chapter in a song, I would borrow the words of this song:

> *"Even when I don't see it you are working.*
> *Even when I don't feel it you are working*
> *You never stop, you never stop working.*
> *You never stop, you never stop working."*

Key Lessons

- Every new level God would get us to will be through the hands and feet of other humans like you. God can use people and events get us to where He wants us to be. The sovereign and miraculous acts of God are always without question. The "gift of men.

- Putting God first brings God into your situation. He adds every other thing to you which others strive and struggle to get.

- Protocols are man-made barriers erected to keep certain unqualified people out. God has His special way of removing those barriers to prove a point. You can trust Him to make the miraculous happen in your career, life and family too.

Chapter Five

31st of May

MY PASSWORD

31ST MAY, MY PASSWORD

I determined never to stop until I had come to the end and
achieved my purpose.

- David Livingstone

very day is the same; we have 24 hours, the sun rises and sets, we have conversations with our loved ones and then another day breaks.

However, each day can be different depending on what you do. Really, not every day should be the same when goals are set and dreams are in motion.

If there is one principle that has changed many lives, it is the fact that we each make our days - we make our days count. It is in one moment that our lives are really changed, it is in one moment we receive that offer, promotion or shift which we've always desired.

I set my heart as a flint...

While I bring my A game to the workplace, I often eat the humble pie when it comes to playing" politics" or lobbying to get ahead. This is neither a good or bad thing, it depends on each person's definition.

I've always rested in the providence of God and His purpose. Every organization is not without its bottlenecks and challenges, and we have to adapt and keep on improving as time goes on. I had begun to think about leaving my miraculous job.

My life cycle had changed and I wanted more. This time no longer from pressure of comparing myself to my friends, more from a knowing that I wanted something more. And so like I always did, I bowed my heart in prayers and asked the Lord for the next step, the next phase to open up.

To put substance to my faith, I changed my password for my system to May 31 of the year 2014. That was the date I really wanted to leave where I worked at the time. So many life's decisions were tied to this next move and I felt like I needed it like the flower needs the rain.

I prayed for this next move each time I logged into my system I reminded God, providence, the universe that this was my deadline. At this time I was only as close as the desire in my heart for a change, nothing had moved in the physical. I pressed on, praying, searching, asking.

When the call came in for another exciting offer, I was excited and my faith was boosted in no little measure. I needed to make my exit by May 31st as I had prayed and so I followed up physically to ensure this.

On the 31st of May in that year this was still a prayer point but only till about 2pm when I got the much awaited call.

As soon as I collected the Offer of Employment letter for a new role, I handed in my letter to my then current organization and that began a new experience entirely. May 31st had become a reality, a change date, a landmark in my life.

What did I learn from that?

Being specific about your requests and desires can determines success. Being clear about your desires a plus. Laser like focus coupled with rugged faith births unusual miracles.

Key Lessons

- Having laser-like focus is a game changer. Is there a goal you are working towards? A desire you want to see fulfilled? Step out in faith. Turn your wish into a plan of action and a matter to speak to God in prayer about.

- A dream without a date is only a wish. Put a date to your desires and work tenaciously towards them. Life only paves a way for those who know where they are going.

CHAPTER SIX

Your CAREER TOOLBOX

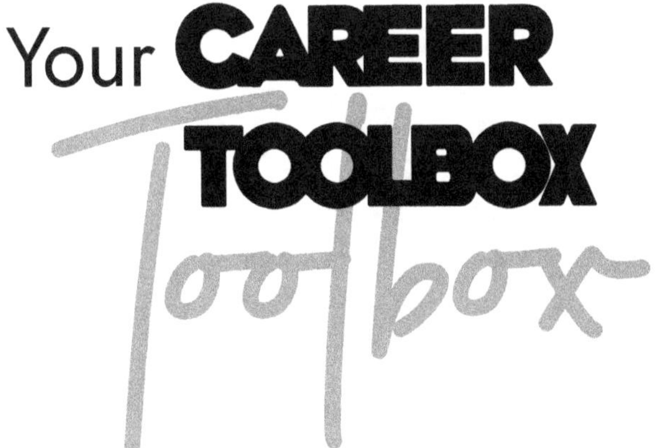

YOUR CAREER TOOLBOX

"Perfection is not attainable, but if we chase perfection we can catch excellence."

- Vince Lombardi

Every occupation has its own unique sets of tools. The chef, engineer, and the CEO all have tools stored up in their tool box. In this chapter, I will be opening up the tools that should be in your Career Toolbox if you desire to ascend the ladder of career success and business leadership.

The first tool in your tool box is:

CHARACTER:

Were you expecting me to start with something high sounding and off-the-hook?

We'll get to other tools in a moment. Character is the foundation for everything. It is why as an HR professional, we will hire a teachable individual that has the basic skills needed for the role, than the cocky and over-the-top person who feels they have the answer to all the world's problems. Character either amplifies your confidence and qualifications or waters it down entirely. Your character says more about who you are than the Curriculum Vitae in your hands or the amazingly written profile on LinkedIn or Wikipedia. It's that important.

Billy Graham, one of the world's greatest evangelist, said, "When wealth is lost, nothing is lost; when health is lost, something is lost; when character is lost, all is lost.

If you are reading this, I believe you have a dream or at least a desire to take leaps forward on your path to career success, I must tell you that your character will be tested along the way.

Abraham Lincoln once said "Nearly all men can stand adversity, but if you want to test a man's character, give him power." Every position you arrive at will come with some measure of power and influence over people.

As I've grown in my pursuits, I've remained constantly aware and conscious as to my reason for being there.

My quest for growth isn't to dominate people, amass wealth to myself or to achieve a status to show off to others - that shouldn't be your motivation too. The purpose for which God keeps promoting me and putting me in positions to lead and coordinate - sometimes small multitudes of people - in the workforce is to that I can bring out the best in them and hopefully add value to them in every way I can as God grants the opportunity to me.

"Character" in the words of Kylie Briscoe "is the aggregate of a person's ethical and moral qualities, and it is demonstrated through the choices we make."

People with character are compassionate, trustworthy, full of integrity, disciplined, and of course, respectful. These are not fancy words to throw around on your resume, they are values to be upheld in the workplace - and everywhere else we find ourselves.

When I think about character, the analogy of a car comes readily to mind. Imagine you have a brand new car (Imagine any favorite brand of yours). It's new, it's fueled up and ready to go.

When you come out on the streets, heads are turning as they admire the vehicle as you drive by with the sun reflecting off the glass. That's good, isn't it? What if your driver loses a nut or two and decides to swerve off the lane, speed off and eventually hit an oncoming vehicle? What happens? There's an accident and people are panicking, arguments break out and there's traffic everywhere.

In the workplace, character determines everything. I am big on competence (I'll share on this next) and a big believer in adding the value that is required to get the job done at the highest level of excellence possible.

Having a "good car" is great, but I should drive "my car" without cutting others off in traffic, using cuss words or breaking traffic rules on the way to my destination.

Your values, words, and disposition to others - ultimately, how you care for others - will determine how far you go.

How is your character? How is your career character?

When you recognize someone who doesn't have principles, shows nasty behavior, and has multiple personalities — step away."

~ Darius Foroux

COMPETENCE

Competence means you have the ability to do something well – your ability to carry out a task effectively.

Your competence can be as simple as developing a client onboarding process to being able to lead and direct a global corporation.

Every organization has its own competency framework with which each member of staff is measured against.

In fact, recruitment is also based on this internal competency framework.

My use of competence here is a compound word that best describes the sum total of: behavior, relevant skills, meeting organizational goals, conforming to organizational standards of excellence, personal performance, and how well a person adapts to company culture.

In today's fast-paced and rapidly changing world, being on the cutting edge of developments in one's field is non-negotiable.

We must constantly be looking out for new information and learning the best practices in the world. This can be made easier by attending events where stakeholders meet and building relationships with men and women who have established a footing in that path.

It's been over two decades of my own professional journey and in these years, I've moved across different industries and roles that were entirely new to me. My friends and colleagues never cease to be amazed at how I am able to pull my weight in every role and bring my very best to it.

Competence is Non-negotiable. I had to enroll for two masters programs along the way. I had already completed my LLM because I studied Law as my First Degree, but when I started working in the Human Resources capacity, I realized that I needed to be schooled so I went for a Master's degree in International Human Resource management. This singular step I took increased my capacity to execute and more importantly, my confidence level grew.

The reality is, there is nothing you cannot do or cannot become.

The brain has been wired to continue to expand by every new knowledge and experience we expose ourselves to. The fact that you studied a certain course in the University or began working in a particular field does not mean that is the only expression there is or can be of you! Your potential is unlimited and uncapped. I already said it, that I am a firm believer that there can be multiple expressions of one person.

New roles come with new demands, and those demands are to stretch you into new dimensions.

BE AN EXECUTION ADDICT

Ideas are everywhere. Almost everyone can provide 10000 ways to solve a problem, but only a few will be willing to roll up their sleeves to get the job done.

Being a calm and observant person, I've sat in several board meetings some were quickies and others lasted longer, and seen how lots of people do the talking, but when it comes to the doing, all hands are no longer on deck. People pass the buck until it lands on table of the one who can get the job done - the one who is not all talk, but big on execution.

I have won awards, at different times for being very strong on execution and I have also been recognized for managing people effectively. You need to build the skills to execute. It goes nicely with the skills to plan! It is the next level that births strategy.

Do not be an idea junkie or a person whose expertise is only in thinking up ideas and suggesting things to be done. Put your hand to the plough always.

To become effective at execution, you have to build laser-like focus directed at your goals. The likelihood of accomplishing a task will be greatly reduced if you have too many things to do at the same time. This is why multi-tasking can be counter-productive if channeled wrongly. You only end up doing so many things without actually getting anything done. Focus on the one thing you need to accomplish in your role, split this into quarterly, monthly, weekly and daily targets. This way, in the long run, you would have achieved more than people who only execute when they feel like or react to every matter that comes to their table.

YOU NEED TO EVOLVE

The key to unlock your future is found in a never ending commitment to learning – this includes professional training and personal development.

The reality is, eventually as you rise on the career ladder, you will arrive at a point where execution takes on a different dimension. Where execution is to be achieved through people and no longer through your hands.

I found this difficult initially because I have always been a hands-on person wanting to do the work no one else was willing to do. However, that had to change, my task was now to ensure others got the job done and this required a different set of skills and competence.

To grow and succeed in this career journey, there is a need to evolve. If you've worked in an organization for 10 years, who you were and what you were capable of at the beginning should be far less than what you are capable of now. Your ability to get things done as at when due and at the level of excellence expected is invaluable in the workplace.

In the words of Shavon Brown, "Continued learning provides a cushion that you can always build on to be innovative and creative. It keeps you abreast of changes and ignites your mental agility."

FIND YOUR TRIBE

In most organizations there are little groups, circles, and caucuses that always have an agenda or a certain kind of mindset they are pushing for. When new entrants come into the organization, they are often tipped to move with a certain click or the other. That's not the point here. No one is truly independent.

We are all dependent on others in some way. By finding your tribe, you leverage the strength of a group rather than your own individual strength.

People who climb the career ladder quickly are those who know how to build rapport and relationships within an organization.

This is not done in a manipulative way to curry some favors or some advantage over others within the organization. Rather it comes from a genuine desire to succeed in your role and also to see the furtherance of the mission of the overall organization. If people cannot get along with you, they cannot go along with you.

CONSTANT LEARNING

Excelling in your career demands a willingness to learn. Irrespective of the university you graduated from or the degrees you've acquired, you would soon be obsolete if you do not add to what you already have.

The world in which we work has grown increasingly complex. New ways of tackling problems are evolving by the second. Staying abreast with the latest developments in your field is the least you can do. Learning is an indispensable tool in your kit. Really, learning doesn't mean loading up the mind with every information that crosses your line of sight. For a broader understanding, to learn first requires unlearning certain methods and way of going about tasks, then, learning and also relearning constantly.

The mind is unlimited and can stretch to any limits you are

willing to go. An unusual career growth will be tied to an unusual investment and sacrifice to learn and grow. There will never really be a favorable time to do anything, you just have to make time to accomplish the goals you set to learn.

There is a reason organizations now have a separate department called Learning and Development. They are to attract and retain top talents, developing the talents within the organization, and also providing motivation to keep the workforce productive.

According to McKinsey, "One of L&D's primary responsibilities is to manage the development of people—and to do so in a way that supports other key business priorities."

The global workforce having experienced drastic changes in the past 2-3 decades; is evolving faster than it has ever done.

With the increasingly competitive business landscape, more complex problems, and also the digital revolution that has changed the way we work forever, a premium has been placed on skilling up. You cannot afford to be caught in the mix. In a later chapter in this book, I wrote about "Learning to prepare for change"

Do you know the beautiful thing about learning today?

With the advent of technology, you do not need to go the

classroom or meet your teachers in person, the classroom and the teacher can come to you - your living room or your bedroom. Learning has been democratized.

This disruption in learning gives you unlimited access and the monopoly of choice to cherry-pick topics to learn about and skills to develop to make you effective in the workplace.

No matter the industry you currently work in, there are myriads of online resources available for your use.

You only need to locate your most preferred platform of learning, then pace yourself on how you want to go.

You literally have the "remote control" with you. More than ever before, the maxim that "your future is in your hands" holds true.

SEEK AND EMBRACE FEEDBACK

Feedback is the food of champions. Seek feedback for your work. Apart from the general appraisals given from time to time, try to establish a relationship with your superiors so as to get more input and feedback from them.

Feedback aids your improvement. This is why HR Professionals have KPIs and other metrics used to measure employee performance.

It is very likely that in the course of your career journey you'll find men and women who will be unnecessarily mean and nasty to you or generally try to pull you down with their words.

Even if you failed at something (based on a feedback you received) you can actually fail forward. In other words, you can use that feedback to improve and to become a better version of you.

THINK FORWARD, KEEP SCANNING FOR OPPORTUNITIES TO BE MORE

Don't be amongst those who say "As long as it's not broken, there's no need to fix it."

Thinking forward helps position you to seek relevant skills, join associations, seek and certifications and jump on the flight to your next level.

As great as your current employment is, always keep your eyes ahead. While you do amazing and excellent work, don't get too comfortable.

I had reached a certain level of success some may consider enviable, but I remember walking into a building of one of the foremost oil and gas companies in the country and a thought travelled through my mind.

I was so inspired by the scenery, the excellence and the ambience that a desire welled up in my heart for the industry.

It's true that God gives us the desires of our hearts when we delight in him. After our meeting that day in that building. No actually, while the meeting was on going, I quietly strolled to a corner in this 7-star high rise building and muttered a prayer under my breath expressing my heart to God. I wanted a chance to work in that industry.

It wasn't long but I knew my words got to God's desires. I had come to recognize my unusual career covenant with Jehovah.

Thinking ahead helps and keeping your eyes up helps you leverage new opportunities and platforms God may be bringing your way for your growth.

It may be uncharted territory, but it is conquerable.

It is possible to move from a company that's barely getting by to multinational, or even a global corporation. It's possible to transit from working in a commercial bank in Nigeria to working in a Fortune 500 Company. Be on the lookout. Everyone should have a long term vision that points forward.

EMOTIONAL INTELLIGENCE

EQ is by far the most important tool in your toolkit as a career professional or even a business professional.

It is necessary to state here that emotional intelligence does not mean being nice, full of smiles and being happy with everyone and everything. On the contrary, at critical moments, it may require being firm, tough, and demanding accountability or even addressing wrong behavior.

Emotional intelligence is not tied to genes or gender. It is more a product of nurture rather than nature. It can be learned. You can get more emotionally intelligent as you grow.

Emotional intelligence does not also mean being overly "emotional" about everything. By "emotional" I don't mean always bearing your mind and stating your own opinion about all issues around you. On the contrary, it may require you to listen attentively to what is not being said so as to respond appropriately to issues.

Everyone; irrespective of position and portfolio within the workplace, needs to build a skill in emotional intelligence.

Emotional intelligence is fast becoming a core skill HR Managers and recruiting organizations use to evaluate prospects. An Emotionally intelligent employee is more likely to succeed and find working more fulfilling than others who are not.

Companies today are beginning to invest heavily into training their employees on EQ.

According to Jeanne Segal et AL, Emotional intelligence is the ability to understand, use, and manage your own emotions in positive ways to relieve stress, communicate effectively, empathize with others, overcome challenges and defuse conflict.

Are you emotionally intelligent? If you are struggling to connect with people, motivate people to get work done or simply not getting along with others, then it means you have to pay attention to this skill.

These four questions will give you a clearer perspective as to whether you are emotionally intelligent or not:

- Are you self-aware? Are you conscious of your thoughts, your own feelings, and emotions and how they influence your words, disposition and work?

- How well can you manage yourself? If you are unable to manage yourself effectively, managing a team or even functioning in one may prove difficult. Are you able to manage your time, schedule and to-do lists effectively without hurting other areas of your life that are equally important? (E.g. family and faith).

- Are you socially aware of others around you? Are you conscious of how your actions or inactions affect others? Are you also conscious of how the actions, words and behaviour of others in your space, affect you?

- How well do you manage and maintain relationships around you?

Relationship management is at the core of emotional intelligence. Are you able to manage conflicts that may arise in the course of relating with people? Are you able to maintain valuable relationships for a long time or do you easily burn bridges at the slightest appearance of a disagreement on issues?

As my work continued to change, I realized that I needed to learn how to manage my 360 degrees stakeholders; managing up, down and across board. There were people who learnt this early enough in their career, but I learnt that later and as soon as I learnt it, a lot of relationships were sustained. In the first half of my career life, it came naturally.

Personally, I believe it was tied to my friendly, humble disposition. Now, in the later part of my career, I do it from a more strategic point because I realize that I need that to get along. I have become more deliberate in managing and building relationships.

Having read through this chapter, how many of these tools do you have in your Toolbox?

If you fall short of any, what is the reason?

Do you give the excuse that you do not have enough time?

There is time for everything.

How about engaging the time between breaks at work on a daily basis?

Dedicating 10minutes, 30minutes, 1 hour lunch breaks to listening to a lesson, carrying out assignments in a course, or simply reading up on that skill will add up several hours of training and growth for you. Yet, all these happened within your normal work hours.

How about leveraging the time spent commuting to and from work (especially if you are not driving)?

Even if you are driving, your vehicle could become your own

YOUniversity. With many lessons and teachings available in audio format, you can download necessary information into your mind that will help you work effectively. While you may be consciously driving, the unconscious mind is soaking in information and insights that will greatly help you.

For most people in the busy metropolis. Chances that we spend approximately 2 hours daily in traffic are quite high. In a week, that's approximately 10 hours. That time window provides invaluable time to take a leap forward.

How about converting the time spent catching up with the gossips and news from social media platforms that do not directly benefit you in any way?

Most social media platforms have community groups of like minds who give valuable advice, tips, and also provide a network of relationships. If at all your social media presence is important, find such groups and leverage on the opportunities they provide. Interact, share, learn, and contribute to the conversation from time to time.

The point I am making here is, there is time for everything you make time for.

Engage the Pareto principle. The truth remains that 80% of the results you get in your life and career will come from 20% of the activities you do.

These tools explained in this chapter is your 20% which cannot be negotiated with anything.

You have to place a premium on getting these tools and engaging them to produce results for you.

Key Lessons

- Investing in yourself is non-negotiable if you want to experience the unusual.

- Take time to study highly successful people in various fields, they engaged a number or a combination of these tools on their way up. You can too.

CHAPTER SEVEN

Employability, The Global Economy, & OPPORTUNITIES Over

EMPLOYABILITY, THE GLOBAL ECONOMY, AND OPPORTUNITIES

"Perfection is not attainable, but if we chase perfection we can catch excellence."

- Vince Lombardi

One of the critical challenges facing Third World nations today is not necessarily unemployment but employability. Government policies in most developed nations are geared towards reskilling and up-skilling its working population to enable them compete effectively in the global workplace.

It goes without saying that the skills of the 21st century and this new decade differs from that of the last 100 years. That's why I wrote extensively about change in another chapter of this book.

Investopedia defines employability as; *"Employability is the life-long, continuous process of acquiring experience, new knowledge—purposeful learning—and skills that contribute to improving one's marketability for enhancing their potential to obtain and maintain employment through various shifts in the labor market. It is based on a set of individual characteristics."*

Top organizations are like sharks in the ocean seeking for new talents to absorb into their workforce. Some organizations literally poach from within other competing organizations, the skilled individuals they desire to have on board. While the challenge of employability is real and daunting, it can be surmounted by getting abreast with information, opportunities and platforms for personal and professional growth. If there is anything life has taught every one of us, it is that we can keep on growing, learning and improving. The room for improvement is one room that can never get filled –there is always room for more.

The Global Economy

There is such a term as "Global Economy" if you are employed, running your business, or on the board of corporation, you are a part of that global economy. As at the time of this writing, the estimation of the worth of the global economy is $88 trillion dollars. The United States is the highest contributor to the global economy boasting 24%, trailing behind them is China and other first world nations.

Why is this important to this book – and to you the reader?

You are a direct contributor to the global marketplace. Through the work that you do, the value that you bring to the workplace, you are putting your nation on the map. The greater the productivity and innovation in a country, the higher the value of its value in the global space.

This is why employability is extremely important. There is a need to consistently reinvent yourself to stay competitive in this trillion dollar global economy.

Global Opportunities

In this $88 trillion dollar economy, opportunities open up globally for people to move into new positions, role, and even businesses expand to new countries. Irrespective of your current location, career opportunities, when seized, could land you in a top global corporation in any part of the world.

You may be asking "How do I find or qualify for opportunities such as these?"

First, do not be a loner in your profession. At the start of your career and even as you go along, you must continue to look at the horizon for opportunities within your organization and outside. There are other corporations looking to hire skilled and result-driven individuals to add value to their company –you could be their next target. Something as simple as learning a new language – for example French, Spanish, Portuguese, can open you up to a new world of opportunities you never knew.

ON EMPLOYABILITY

"While Nigeria's unemployment rate has climbed to 27.1% (up from 23.1 in Q3 2018, when the unemployment report was last published), the country's underemployment rate- which reflects those working less than 40 hours a week, or in jobs that underutilize a person's skills, time, or education- has increased to 28.6%."

That excerpt is what pops up when you input, "Statistics of unemployment in Nigeria" on Google. A further peek into the full article, the writer wrote:

"…with a labor force of 80.2 million, that means about 21.7 million Nigerians are unemployed, a figure that exceeds the population of 35 of Africa's 54 countries."

Just before you think Nigeria is deep in trouble, it is important to know that the problem of unemployment is not peculiar to the Giant of Africa but in the evolving world, unemployment is fast becoming a global challenge.

The reason is not to be far-fetched, the use of technology in sync with government policies, have caused the marginalization of human capital and labour. Thereby causing a drop in the demand of the latter. Employers are out to seek human resources who have the exact requisite skills to be a part of the company or organization's work force.

This begs the question, "Is unemployment caused by the unavailability of jobs or the incapability of human resources?

Someone provided an answer to this when she said, "Youth unemployabilty is a greater challenge than youth unemployment."

Her statement underscores the fact that- structural unemployment is a result of workers' lack of essential skills, which leads to a contrast between the demands of employers and the employees' offer.

Employability is the ability of an individual to gain and maintain employment. It encompasses the skills - technical, soft, hard and transferable skills - that enables and empowers an individual to be gainfully employed.

Terence Chew puts it this way, "Employability is the ability to enthrall employers with undisputable capabilities to optimize personal development and job growth."

In that light, it is crystal clear that unemployment and unemployability are two different concepts. And, while it is almost normal for one to be unemployed, it is a total disaster to be unemployable. The ease with which you become employed is dependent on how employable you are.

On my career journey, like I recounted in other parts of this book, I was in-between jobs at different points in time. However, at every point, I gave myself to learning and the process of evolution. I garnered skills that put me forward as being highly employable. My employability was very imperative to the ease with which I accessed top companies and rose through the ranks.

At a time I held a lower position at a company but as time went by, my immediate boss recommended me for a higher role. Of course, that was another unusual event on my career journey, and I attribute it to God. But, you will recall that I earlier mentioned how I studied and prepared myself for every position. In essence, while you pray, you must work too.

How then can you harness your potentials to make yourself employable and compete in the ever raging talent war in the world?

Many are of the opinion that educational degrees and academic statuses are the yardsticks to measure employability. Even America's First Black President, Barack Obama, once said,

"With the changing economy, no one has lifetime employment. But, community colleges provide lifetime employability."

Conversely, with the fast evolving world of technology and the dynamism of the global economy, that school of thought has had to come under fire. Times and seasons tell us that in today's world you need more than an educational degree to find your rightful place in the work force.

Take for instance, when there is a job opening, several people submit their curriculum vitae. It won't be surprising to find individuals who have studied the same course in the same institution and even graduated with the same grades, apply for the same job. But, what gives Mr. A an edge over Mr. B?

It is their employability status which is a sum total of technical, hard, soft and transferable skills; many of which would not have been acquired in the four walls of an educational institution.

This, nonetheless, is not to rule out the importance of educational degrees. Unequivocally, the academic curriculum, co-curriculum and extra-curriculum offer values that are contributory to the employability of a person.

In reiteration, one's employability is affected by the employability of others when seeking a specific job. Hence, the need to acquire all the skills relevant to your career and job.

I will highlight some of these skills according to the different categories they belong to:

HARD SKILLS

Otherwise called 'Technical skills', according to investopedia.com, these are skills and knowledge necessary for effective participation in the work force. They are tangible and specific to certain tasks or activities. In other words, these are skills that are acquired to carry out precise duties and they are relative to special or well defined functions.

They include (but not limited to); being bilingual or multilingual, database management, mobile development, user interface design, marketing campaign management, effective use of mathematics, programming languages, data mining, statistical analysis, SEO/SEM marketing, and many others.

It is worthy of note that you do not need to have all of these, their acquisition is highly dependent on their relevance to your job in relation to the global workplace.

Many times, people get intimidated by the grandiloquence nature of the names these skills are called but a closer study of what they entail draws you closer to being employable. These skills may or may not be taught in formal academic settings, but their use is essentially applicable in an area of the work force.

Also, it is one thing to acquire these, it is a different ball game entirely to develop them. Our world is constantly undergoing evolution, hence, what is in trend today, could be outdated tomorrow. Bearing that in mind, you must avoid obsolescence by giving yourself to relentless learning.

SOFT SKILLS

These are non-technical skills and they are basically personal traits which comprises of work ethics, enthusiasm to work, sense of responsibility, emotional intelligence, cultural competence, attention to detail, critical thinking, effective communication, teamwork, problem solving, adaptability, empathy, integrity, open-mindedness, amongst several others.

These set of skills are inculcated by individuals and they play a key role in employability. They go beyond what you write in your CV, or the qualities you listed in the qualifying essays; they are the attributes that you give off after your hard skills must have earned you a job.

Remember, employability is not just gaining employment, but sustaining employment too. So, the efficiency of your technical skills does just a part, sustainability is built upon your soft skills. The amusing thing about soft skills is that they cannot be falsified, they give you away at every opportunity. Thus, be intentional about how you lead your life, the values you hold in high regard and your attitude generally.

TRANSFERABLE SKILLS

Like the name rightly connotes, these are skills that can be transferred across diverse facets of the labor market. They are skills that can be applied in different types of professions or jobs. Simply put, a skill that is applicable in the tech world could also come in handy in the banking industry. How is that possible?

Transferrable skills share a border with soft skills and they could be considered mutually inclusive. Transferable skills include work experience, intellectual capabilities and achievements, social skills, etc. In contrast to that, non-transferable skills are limited to a particular field, thereby restricting the employability of individuals.

In essence, employers look out for the combination of these skills when assimilating new workers. Whichever part of the labour force you belong to, blue-collared or white-collared, your ability to continuously upgrade your skills, do not just give you an edge over your contemporaries, it increases your employability status.

CHAPTER EIGHT

IT'S OVER

IT'S OVER

"Never give up, for that is just the place and time that the tide will turn."

Harriet Beecher Stowe

A certain biblical character, Hagar, was exiled from Abraham's house at a critical time in her life. On her journey, their provision was exhausted and there was no one to help. Amidst the lack and fatigue, she must have hsaid to herself 'It's over' too many times to count. Her mental and physical strength were exhausted. Her fighting spirit was deflated and death looked like the next best thing for her.

She couldn't bear to watch her child die so she sat far away from him and kept on sobbing.

We all get to crossroads in life where going forward looks impossible and going backwards is unthinkable. Strangely at those points, the heavens may even seem like brass and you'll find yourself saying, "God, just make a way again" or like Samson, "Give me strength one more time."

I was offered an expatriate consulting role outside Nigeria for the next company I worked for. Notice I said "Offered" because by now you know the drill, I didn't ask for this or position for this in any way but I got the opportunity. This was unusual and rapid as I had just joined the organization few months before. The meteoric rise astounded everyone too but then, its career unusual, life unusual too.

After spending some time in the expatriate role, I returned to my home country to continue working and then Two major shifts happened with me. The loss of a loved one (my sister) and the need to change career at the time. Let's just say this was occasioned by the circle of life.

It was one of the most painful moments of my life and career journey.

There were murmurs, what next for her? Is this the end?

Maybe the murmurs were true. Maybe they were in my mind. I sure as heaven felt them.

During this break in my career journey, I decided to go deeper I my walk with God. . I had always allowed the excuse of work and not having enough time keep me from going deeper, but after I left my job at the beverage manufacturing company where I worked for about 2 years, , I decided to focus on God a little bit more, since I didn't have the demands of a job or babies I was raising. I enrolled in a Bible School and I finished all the levels I had to and of course you can't do that and your life won't change for the better. Gradually my prayer life improved dramatically and my grasp of the things of God got better. From this point on, I learned how to maximize the middles.

Sometimes when we think we have reached the end of the road, a little look further will reveal that it was just a bend. God often uses challenges to nudge us into deeper fellowship and communion with Him. This is by far a higher calling than any offer letter any company could give to us.

I didn't think I was a good prayer warrior on my own so anywhere I hear of a prayer meeting, I would attend because I felt that was the only way I could build my prayer life. I just kept on attending and that was how I became better at it and I continued going higher and higher because I was actively involved with God.

Key Lessons

· Nothing is really over until you throw in the towel. As long as breathe still flows in and out of your nostrils and blood through your veins, there is a way out of where you currently are. Your end is meant to be "an expected end" not a journey that was cut short. Keep hoping for the best.

·Tragedy and loss are a part of life. Knowing how to manage one's emotions and find new meaning to these life events will make a difference in how our lives eventually turn out. It is not what happens to us that really matters, but how we respond to it.

· In moments when all hell may seem to break loose, God may be calling you into something deeper – a call to intimacy and deepening of your communion with Him.

Quirky Thoughts

What we mask

I am curious to see how many likes a picture will get.

I needed to dash out for a meeting and so I put on a scarf, but to everyone outside, that was all they could see.

I needed to be at this meeting so all I had to do was to mask the "untidiness" underneath.

My thoughts then went to how beautiful everything can appear on the surface while we mask so much underneath.

If you're masking anything underneath, I must commend your strength. But please, know when it is time unveil, to exhale, and to let it all out.

Know when to unmask and admit you need help.

Pleasure and pain are all a part of life.

Have you ever masked your pain so much that when it

turned around and you were celebrating, no one really understood the magnitude of the win because you never really expressed the pain anyway?

It can be an anti-climax!

You need your pain for your pleasure.

It is even a bigger disappointment on its own to be jubilating over something no one understands but rather everyone feels it is no big deal.

How do you express the victory if you ever told of the war?

When we do this, we miss the opportunity to really grow from the pain.

Yes, go through the process victoriously but leave room to acknowledge the challenge. It makes the win so much sweeter for you and for your cheerleaders rooting for you.

As for my hair that day, the masking lasted all for 4 hour as my hair needed to breathe.

I got home and washed it out right after my meeting.

CHAPTER NINE

Your JOB, CALLING, PURPOSE

YOUR JOB, CALLING, PURPOSE

"It's not enough to have lived. We should be determined to
live for something."

- Winston S. Churchill

Russian *Storyteller and essayist,* Fyodor Dostoyevsky, once said, "The mystery of human existence lies not in just staying alive but in finding something to live for."

What's a life without purpose?

It did not take me very long to realize that securing a good job or working in the foremost organizations wasn't an end in itself – but a means to an end.

Whether you work in a glass office or in the Oval office, there is much more to your presence there than the accolades and comfort you enjoy. You may, from your glass office, bask in the sheer beauty of the landscape that you see, but what matters more is how you can respond to the needs of the people you meet and touch every life that God allows into your circle of influence.

Come to think of it, once we get on that career train, it continues for the rest of our lives.

Annie Dillard, a writer, once said, "How we spend our days is, of course, how we spend our lives." For most of us, our days are spent at work. You will agree with me that the common denominator within the workplace and outside is people. People are everywhere.

Purpose is all about touching lives irrespective of whatever context we find those people.

Research reveals that we spend a whopping 90,000 hours of our lives at work. That's a large chunk of life gone already. Shouldn't we make that count for more than meeting deadlines, running into meetings, and earning a fat paycheck?

I realized early enough that all I was given was to be a tool in God's hands to achieve His ultimate purpose for me.

I would not be like the ungrateful-self-absorbed-Babylonian king who thought his empire was totally a product of his wits, intelligence, and strength.

Without a doubt, my career path – and that of everyone else – should never be an end in itself, it is a vehicle going somewhere.

It is one thing to find a job, it is another to find a calling. It is even more fulfilling when your calling (or life's work and assignment) is in direct alignment with the job you already do. Being stuck in a job you hate because you love the pay is a recipe for a life of unfulfilment.

It's one beautiful thing to be alive, making a living and breathing just fine; but, it is a different boat cruise to live life to its fullest.

You will agree that when a child is born, we can always tell what turn its life will take. First, a few years into life, that baby gets enrolled in the kindergarten class. Then, all the way through the nursery school and up to the basic primary school.

In most developing nations, at age 9-10, a child is preparing for secondary school. At age 15-16, the higher institution comes calling. Under normal circumstances and with all things being equal, the child should be done with a first degree at 22years.

The next step is to seek for a job to earn a living, after all, the whole idea of schooling is to garner enough knowledge to earn money. Then comes marriage and raising a family. You work your back off to keep the family together and for a large part of your life, you are stuck with a work schedule. In a twinkle of an eye, you are hitting retirement age and if you worked for the government, you'll live off your pension and – like most African parents believe – eat the fruit of your labour through your children. You live like this till the inevitable happens- DEATH.

This is the regular cycle of life and many people are diligently following it. But, is that all there is to life? School. Work. Family. More Work. Retirement. Death.

Of course not!

Humans were created for many things and this cycle does not do justice at all. How will you express the gifts, talents, potentials and skills you have been blessed with by sticking to this rigid routine? They must go into something and your existence should not be like the snake who walked the hills without prints.

In the words of Winston S. Churchill, "It's not enough to have lived. We should be determined to live for something." This implies that, every breath you take should count and give life to someone else. Your life should be lived for a purpose because when God created man, it was for a purpose; and this purpose must come into reality.

So, what's your purpose? What do you live for? Why do you live? Who or what is affected by your existence? What will you be remembered for? What is the true essence of the life you live?

Suffering a career break yet again after over a decade of smooth fast rising career took me back to my initial career journey. This time, being older and wiser, I did not just want to jump back into the career band wagon. I wanted to find career purpose. So Two things drove my next move, my desire to make an impact and help people, my love for the entertainment industry and remember I had asked God for an opportunity in oil and gas? So let's see how those played out.

There is this joy I derive in helping people and it would be safe to say, I am obsessed with helping people.

I commit myself to helping people, especially total strangers, get a job placement without having any connection to anybody at the top. The thoughts of lending a helping hand to someone keeps me awake at night and it drives me at every point of my career. I strongly believe that as I rise in my career path, I am to help other people rise too.

I am simply that person who never wants to see others get hurt and I am an advocate of a fair, right and balanced life. As you journey along the path of purpose, you will encounter all kinds of people: the envious, the ones who are out to take from you, and the ones who are truly God-sent. I had my own fair share of these experiences.

I'll rather have the complexities and challenges that come with a life of purpose than go through life idle and pursuing self-satisfaction.

A life without purpose can be likened to a doughnut with a hole -it's not just complete. Many times, we try to run away from fulfilling purpose, there are many times we pretend not to see what God is pointing us to and then we shut our eyes to it. Other times, we know and are very convinced about what we have been called to do, but the desires of our heart and excuses we make up for ourselves take the better part of us.

(I have put a series of questions at the end of this chapter that will help channel your attention and give you direction regarding answering this purpose question)

You will often hear people say, "Why me?", "Why should I be the one to do this?" "Am I the only one to do this, can't someone else just do it?"

Here is the bubble buster:

There are many other people out there who will do just what you don't want to do. There are several other vessels ready for the Lord's use and if you do not make yourself available, God will raise other men. If you and I relent or refuse to live up to God's expectations, there are over 7 billion other people He can use. It is a rare privilege to walk this earth fulfilling the very agenda for why we were sent here.

If you feel God is laying an idea in your heart, you can be sure that there are other people receiving the same instructions too. The sad thing is this- if you do not act accordingly and at the right time, you might lose out on the blessings attached to that. On a larger scale, if you do not live out your purpose, you will have to deal with the emptiness that comes with purposeless living.

I have discovered that meeting people's needs is not just something I enjoy doing and have a passion for, but therein lays my purpose.

During the years of my career break and growth, I had tightened up as it relates to giving, if you get my drift. I was conserving resources, but I was uncomfortable.

So, in this period of a career break, I prayed to God for forgiveness and restoration. I tied my career come back to my purpose to be a source of help. I dared to dig inside for my passion and ask for an opportunity in this and for good measure, I threw in my desire to work in the oil and gas sector. Its God remember? I have an unusual career covenant remember? If only you believe, remember?

Knowing I have a calling to Help, I decided not to worry about where resources will come from. Remember the statement I made to my parents when I was younger? My spending was over the roof back then, but now, my spending had become attached to a lofty purpose.

It is God's responsibility to provide the wealth while I remain the channel for its disbursement. I am not claiming to be an embodiment of wealth. I am claiming that for the purpose God needs me to accomplish, He has put the resources within reach for me, for that purpose.

Many of us burden ourselves with the worry of 'How to fulfil purpose'.

The excuse we make up usually centers on what we lack and not on what we have. The simple truth is this: God will never send you on a mission without equipping you. We all have the potentials necessary to fulfil purpose. We just have to be strategically positioned and ready for use.

Like Paul, I forget the things which are behind and pressed towards higher things. I honed my skills and worked in the right direction which ultimately increased my capacity, income and influence.

Remember, I had pursued a career in the legal profession before transiting to HR. I strongly believe it was divinity at work. I took a course in HR which qualified me as an HR expert. So, when God was bringing job opportunities my way, I could easily fit in with my qualifications. Even though, I must admit that God's grace qualified me more than certifications.

The inspiration of God cannot be overruled in the place of purpose discovery and fulfilment. I have come to see God as the one who sends you on an errand and supports you with everything you will need to deliver successfully. I have gotten job opportunities I shouldn't have and accessed places I couldn't have ordinarily. Having a regular job which God blessed me with, provided me the resources needed to make the impact I wanted and still want to make.

I set up a youth empowerment program in my hometown. I wanted the people to connect with the world, so I enabled this through the establishment of an internet parlor, named after my late father.

My focus with this was to reach out to people. Despite the criticisms that came with that, I did not let that stop me, purpose had to be fulfilled and I was on a mission to do that.
I find fulfilment when I see lives being touched and I spread this

heart to everyone around me regardless of what life throws at me. The simple truth is that, for everyone on a journey, you will meet roadblocks. The path that leads to fulfilling purpose is not void of thorns but you are not void of strength either.

I had found my voice and I am putting it to good use.

Just like I was, there are many people out there who are not fulfilling purpose because they have made the life of others a blueprint of theirs. You will find people running the race of others, thereby neglecting their own lane. We often forget that, just as our faces are unique, our purposes are too. You can never be called to be the same person as another person, not even your identical twin. There is a place of self-discovery in purposeful living.

Allow me paint a scenario to you. Imagine, two friends- one has a pen and the other has a knife. The pen is used to write and the knife is used to cut and, or slice, right? Now, imagine, the friend with a pen trying to use his pen to cut oranges, just because his friend with a knife does it effortlessly. Two things are bound to happen: He will not only injure the orange and himself, but the effort will end up in futility.

That is exactly what we do when we try to live like others. The purpose walk cannot be successful if you are living someone else's life.

A Greek Philosopher once said, "Knowing yourself is the beginning of wisdom." And the Bible affirmed in the book of Proverbs that, "Wisdom is the Principal thing." So, if we would blend these thoughts, we could say, "Knowing yourself is the Principal thing."

The journey to discovering purpose starts with the knowing of who you are. The journey is inwards.

"As human beings, we're wired to connect, and part of purpose is serving others or serving the greater good, something outside of us that allows us to feel more connected."

- Jacinta Jimenez

When in the end I take a walk from the corporate world to venture fully into the new dreams of my heart in the entertainment industry, I would not only be proud of the many awards, accolades, and applause I received. I would be more grateful and fulfilled that I stood as ambassador and channel of blessing and upliftment to many people I was privileged to come across all through my over two decades of work.

Personal evaluation questions on purpose

1. Who am I?

2. Where do I come from?

3. What can I really do?

4. Why am I here?

5. Where am I going?

6. Where do I see myself going?

7. What gives me the greatest joy when I do it?

Notes

Key Lessons

- The essence of life is purpose. A life without purpose is not worth living.

- Your job or the work that you do is a field where the purpose of God for you can also be accomplished.

Become comfortable with being uncomfortable

I have had to learn to become comfortable with being uncomfortable.

I've always been able to make unpopular decisions and stand by them if that's my conviction. Maybe it comes with age? Maybe it comes with knowing who you are better.

As you read this, reflect.

You may find something surprising about yourself.

Here's a quote I love; I believe you will too:

"Some people say you are going the wrong way when it is simply a way of your own."

Can you relate?

CHAPTER TEN

Learn to INITIATE CHANGE

LEARN TO INITIATE CHANGE

"Avoid the temptation of getting comfortable. The hungry eat first."

-Kirk Franklin

*B*y *the time you are done reading this chapter,* your hair would have grown 1.1 inches longer than it is right now, you would have blinked more than 20 times, and you would have breathed in air more than 30 times as your heart mixes blood with oxygen to keep you up.

As a matter of fact, your heart – that never-tiring-machine – would have beat more than 100 times.

Somewhere around the world, 300,000 tons of ice would have collapsed in the Antartica as the glaciers are melting at a rate three times faster than the last decade; and not surprising, over 5 million searches would have been completed on Google.

What am I driving at?

Life is always on motion.

Change is constant.

Everything changes – even if you do not notice; everything is moving.

Change, in the words of a philosopher, is the only permanent thing in life – it is the only thing that never changes.

Change!

It defines everything in the universe. Without change you won't be where you are today, you won't even be reading this right now. Imagine you didn't "change" from being a baby to being an adult; imagine you never learned to read and write, you won't understand a thing about what you are looking at right now. You changed along the way and that's why you are who you are, and where you are currently.

Contrary to what many think, change isn't only what happens to us, it is also what we can make happen. The many books I've read were written by someone, the countries I have travelled to, were built by individuals; the amazing relationships I share with friends and family was intentionally created.

I have evolved from that young lady who was trying to figure out life and to find her first job to this woman who can now teach, inspire and help others become better versions of themselves and to really be an example to others.

The late Dr. Myles Munroe – in his book Principles of Change – wrote about 4 kinds of change; and I find them instrumental to what I intend to share in this chapter.

Here:

- Change that happens around you

- Change that happens to you

- Change that happens within

- Change that we make happen

While I do not take credit for the entire miraculous and sudden shifts in my life, I could trace everything to desire – the desire to be more, do more, and help more people.

I do not attribute the changes in my life entirely and many transitions in my own life entirely to my own effort – but if there is one thing I have a strong detest for; it is failure.

The desire to not fail is always strong enough to propel me towards succeeding at whatever my hands find to do. This is what led me to give my "all" when I was building from the scratch at the start of my career.

Ever heard of the characters: Sniff, Scurry, Hem, and Haw?

One of the most influential books of the last 20 years was written by Spencer Johnson. It is the famous Who moved my cheese? Little wonder he has sold over 20 million copies globally.

Change! That's the concept he so wittingly and comically explained using the characters: Sniff. Scurry. Hem. Haw

In a moment, you will find out who you are amongst the characters.

Sniff and Scurry are little mice who are largely ruled by instinct and are quick to respond and are pro-active.

Hem and Haw are little humans – with complex analytic reasoning and cognitive capabilities – much like many of us today.

In the story, these 4 characters loved cheese so much and daily they visited a particular station to feast on the cheese. They found joy, fulfillment, and satisfaction in the cheese daily. Not too long after, Hem and Haw - the little humans - became complacent and didn't notice the cheese was getting exhausted. Sniff and Scurry noticed and were making plans to seek alternatives.

One bright morning, Hem and Haw came to the Station and found it empty.

Alarmed! Hem screamed "Who moved my cheese?"

While Sniff and Scurry were off seeking for better cheese, Hem and Haw were hitting their head against the wall, blaming everyone and expecting things to return to the way they once were.

If there's anything this new decade has taught us, it is things can change...very quickly too.

For every time you lost an opportunity, a loved one, failed a test or go through uncomfortable cycles in life; you may be tempted to ask like Hem and Haw asked; who moved my cheese? Will things ever go back to normal? How do I get my life back on track?

Your "cheese" could be your current job you find so fulfilling and look forward to build a beautiful future.

Your "cheese" could be your desire to move to another country as you build up dreams of a better future in that place.

Your "cheese" could be an opportunity you currently enjoy or you seek to.

In the nature of man, we are not so easy to adapt, change or move into new things.

Nothing happens suddenly. There are often a series of events that are already taking place long term which you may not have been aware of. No company suddenly files for bankruptcy or decides to merge with another.

As a person, you must be able to read the handwriting on the wall each day you show up at work.

The suddenness of change and the discomfort it brings should make you want to prepare for it more than being taken unawares by it. This informed my cry to God to always take me out of organizations when it seemed it was nearing its demise. In every place I have been privileged to work, God showed up for me when the boat was about to sink. He always provided an alternative – a better alternative.

When you find a good opportunity or job placement, perhaps do not build a permanent structure in that place alone. Leave a little room.

From time to time, look on the horizon, ask questions, and equip yourself. You may not really know in which way life's pendulum will swing, but in whichever way it eventually does, if you have anticipated it, you'll be better equipped to respond, rather than react to it.

Have you ever wondered why Abraham – the Patriarch; lived in tents all his life and even his sons? It was because he sought for something bigger, better, and longer lasting. It was a future that was more than a good paycheck, a flock of bleating sheep or mooing cows. He wanted more – and you should too.

To handle change, you have to:

1.   Accept that change is a constant – a fact of life that cannot be removed.

2.   Prepare for change.

3.   Respond, not react, to change.

4.   Having a progressive mindset.

Key Lessons

- Change is inevitable. If you do not initiate change, it will happen to you.

- Anticipating and preparing for change positions you for greater opportunities.

Chapter Eleven

A word to WOMEN

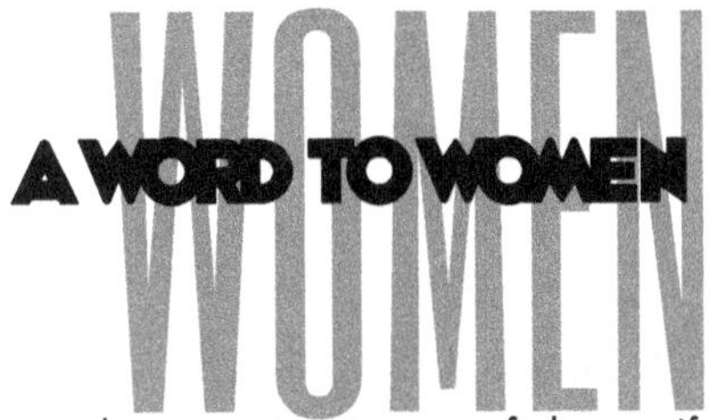

"I believe all women need a support system, a safe haven, if you will, filled with resources as a platform to help them thrive."

Dana Dewedoff-Carney |
Founder, Rise For Women

*I*magine a world where women are free to aspire to the highest *heights possible in any field,* a world where women would not have to be discriminated against due to certain inevitable life transitions like child birth or marriage.

Imagine a world where women are paid what they are worth and are given platforms for unhindered expression in every sphere of influence.

Imagine a world where women are supporting other women selflessly and giving their shoulders for others to ride on.

Imagine a world where women believe in themselves and walk with heels of confidence and pride to take on the beautiful future God designed for them.

That world is possible. Yes, with the effort that you and I put in, there is no limit.

There is no doubt that women have the capacity to lead and create change in the workplace and in every other place they find themselves.

Women are a force the world is yet to explore to the fullest. From research, we see that over the past five years, the number of women in senior leadership positions have grown significantly. However, the level of representation isn't as much as is required to bring great levels of change world over.

I must state here that the narratives and conversations around women globally is not a call for domination or unhealthy comparison with our men, but a heartfelt desire for expression of potential and capacity.

Sheryl Sandberg (Chief Operating Officer, Facebook) and Rachel Thomas said: Companies should do everything they can to make their workplaces more fair—starting with putting best practices in place to get bias out of hiring and promotions. When you take bias out of the equation, women will finally get the equal chance they've always deserved. Everyone will."

More women, according to the United Nations, have entered

political positions in recent years including through the use of special quotas. While this is a welcome development, women still hold a mere 23.7 per cent of government seats, far short of parity.

Also in the Private sector, there is little improvement as women globally occupy less than a third of senior and middle management positions available.

There is a certain glass ceiling that's rather invisible which keeps women from aspiring to the highest heights possible. Society sells a certain narrative to women, and even as women we sometimes doubt our own God-given capacity and genius.

Living the unusual life will require breaking out of social norms and expectations, taking risks, wielding courage as a weapon and leveraging the grace that God provides.

There is no crime in being ambitious, daring, or having a desire to sit at the table where major decisions are made; either in the workplace or even in governance.

What I believe women should do:

Find the right models. Many women are fast rising to the top more than ever in every industry. Find them, learn from them, and get into their network. Find mentors who are passionate about investing in women. Don't allow stereotypes keep you in the status-quo. There are countless women supporting other women. Also, in your little corner of the world, shine your own light and help other women rise. Your shoulder can be all that another woman needs to stand on to become all that she could become.

Encourage other women to aspire to higher positions and platforms of influence.

I believe we are in the age of the rise of powerful women who will shape and change the world.

In a joint session of the United Nations General Assembly in 2016 a set of goals were formed, and cardinal amongst these goals was a direct focus on women and girls.

SDG 5 states: Achieve gender equality and empower all women and girls.

- There is a global outcry and consensus to recognize and value unpaid care and domestic work through the provision of public services, infrastructure and social protection policies and the promotion of shared responsibility within the household and the family as nationally appropriate.

· Ensure women's full and effective participation and equal opportunities for leadership at all levels of decision-making in political, economic and public life.

(Coined from the SDG goals of the UN)

Dear woman, you are not umbilically tied to being average or subservient. Cut the cord if you think you are. It's time to breathe the fresh air of possibilities and opportunities.

I'll end this chapter by giving an echo to the beautiful words of Maya Angelou:

You are a phenomenal women, yes - you.

Key Lessons

Women are valuable. They bring much value to the world and the workplace.

Women need to rise up to the challenge of leadership and to aspire to the highest heights possible.

Quirky Thoughts

I was just thinking that strength of character is really not to be taken lightly.

It is the steel to stand regardless, to stand on the side of your positive conviction, a truth, steadfastness or justice. Sometimes even to self-detriment, but in defense of a deeper truth or cause.

You come out stronger, the process is painful, but you are always vindicated.

Sometimes, when you let go and play the fool, somehow the universe knows and you are replenished and blessed in a deeper and stronger way.

You come out stronger, not involving yourself in the squabbles of men, but in a higher purpose that even you will reflect and know there's a deeper side to life.

So, sometimes it is

"No thank you, but on this, I will pass."

I will not be shallow.

I will not be ephemeral.

I will look to the limit of my nose.

I will look beyond.

In this there is opportunity and there is strength of character.

This is my belief and stance.

CHAPTER TWELVE

ETHICS & YOU

"A man without ethics is a wild beast loosed upon this world."

Albert Camus

*E*thics *refer to a system of principles that govern or determine what is right and wrong.* Wherever there is a gathering of people for a cause, there are ethics expected of such an environment.

Established ethics help to regulate actions, reward alignment to the principles, and also punish bad behavior that doesn't align with the ethics.

The workplace has its own ethics too. For want of a definition, workplace ethics are sets of values, moral codes, and standards to be followed by employers and employees within an organization. These rules are non-negotiable.

In most organizations, these ethics are expressly written and also communicated to new staff once they are recruited into an organization. For most people, these ethics come naturally.'

In this chapter, I'll be talking about the not-too-commonly talked about ethic:

KINDNESS:

So often we are so engrossed in organograms, charts, and work that we forget the most important element in the workplace - people. How we treat people is an ethic that is often overlooked.

People who are high up the line of authority do not see any need to be kind to those who they lead.

I'll like to relate a familiar story here...

A certain man who earned a fat six-figure salary in a Fortune 500 company found a rare opportunity to invest his assets into a new venture that would give him the freedom and independence he always craved.

He quickly resigned and sunk his feet deep into this investment pool without in-depth study, analysis and verification of the claims the investors had brought to him.

Just 4 months after he resigned from this company, this Fortune 500 six figure earning individual, lost all he had. Everything. His money and his assets were completely tied up to the investments he made and the investment company he worked with had vanished into thin air.

He made one quick search on the Nation's company register only for him to realize that the company never existed. He was wounded emotionally, financially, and even his health was beginning to deteriorate. He reached out to his former bosses, but they were all too busy with work to pay him any attention.

He reached out to his Pastor. His pastor made him realize that he couldn't help much because he warned him and besides, he wasn't even regular at church meetings. He reached out to friends but they were all on a 6-month vacation and didn't want to be disturbed.

He seemed to have come to the end of his life.

He was planning to take his life when a random call came in. It was one of the junior staff that worked under him in the former organization.

He called to check on him knowing what had happened. This junior staff offered him a place to stay at his own house for the time being till he could recover from his losses.

Does this story seem too good to be true? I only tried to relate a biblical story using some 21st century scenario.

Jesus told a parable of the man going on a journey from Jerusalem to Jericho when he was accosted by robbers and he was badly injured and near death.

The Scribe with all his knowledge, class, and influence, saw him, shook his head and passed by.

The Priest came by with his regalia and religious position, shook his head pitied him and went on his way...perhaps to preach a fiery sermon in the temple.

All the people who you'll think had the resources, power and influence to cause a change in people's lives did nothing.

A simple Samaritan then came along; we do not know his name, pedigree, academic qualifications or titles; but we see his heart.

He stopped in his tracks, got off his ride, and treated the wounds of this unidentified person. He placed this wounded man on his own ride and took care of him.

Luke.10.34 - And went to him, and bound up his wounds, pouring in oil and wine, and set him on his own beast, and brought him to an inn, and took care of him.

This is unusual. A heart of kindness is everything.

I wrote this to encourage you to bring "Heart" into all that you do.

By "Heart" I mean love - love not just for what you do, but for the people you do life with on a daily basis.

The unusual career life is a career life of unconditional love, kindness, and genuine compassion for others.

This heart of love and compassion has been ingrained in me from as far back as I can remember, perhaps learned from my dad. Perhaps Gods pathway for me

Loving people comes natural, but for some others, effort has to be put into this. Doors are opened to people who open the door for others.

One act of kindness can change your story and that of others as well. Usually, you are never there when your name is mentioned in conversations. It isn't only the great work you do that speaks for you, people also speak for you.

God often uses the people we least expect to accomplish the biggest dreams we may have in our hearts.

The places I've been to, the roles I've filled and opportunities that has come my way, came with very little "workings" on my part.

They were unusual. The turn and twists of events in my life have convinced me that the kindness of God is real...and I must, more importantly, be an extension of His kindness to everyone in my space.

INTEGRITY

First of all, because I'm a Christian, and I upload the values and culture of a believer in Christ. Asides this, the values my father instilled in me and my other siblings still speak today. In a lot of ways I'm like him.

My dad always said, "Kwuba akagi oto" which means to deal uprightly in everything we did. I used this principle of his to speak to an audience in one of the popular universities in South Western Nigeria where I was invited to speak.

Honestly, I never want my name to be in anything that is not straight; and you should too. A good name is more to be desired than silver and gold. I have been involved in projects and jobs where people engage in underground deals but I have constantly distanced myself from such people.

Does it mean I have no desire for more wealth or status? Certainly not. If I come across a clean deal that I deserve in the normal course of things, I get myself involved but to circumvent process, not me.

Integrity was something my dad was known for. He also used to say, rather frequently, in Igbo language (From Eastern Nigeria) "Ihe oma adighi agu agu" which means, "Good things never finish." I believe people who soil their names and are willing to compromise their values suffer from a scarcity mentality. They think only of what to grab in the here and now without thinking of the ripple effect of their actions. You must realize that there's always something fresh coming for you where you are now. You must have integrity as a personal and work ethic.

MUTUAL RESPECT

Respect should be given to all irrespective of age, gender, status, or race. Intrinsically, we are all the same or at least, bear similar characteristics.

Respect is a human virtue that we must uphold.

The timeless maxim of treating others the way you want to be treated cannot be overemphasized.

Showing respect to people creates an environment for cordial relationships to thrive.

Respect will reduce the likelihood of conflict and tension. Even when conflicts arise - which is sometimes inevitable - the issues will be sorted out amicably still in an atmosphere of trust and respect for one another.

In an environment where everyone feels important and respected, the level of productivity will be high. The reality is, no one will function effectively in an atmosphere of conflict and disrespect or an atmosphere where people are constantly exchanging hurtful words and pulling others down.

Mutual respect helps to create a positive culture in the workplace.

PROFESSIONALISM

Professionalism is a lot of things in one. It includes competence, accountability, reliability, punctuality, self-control. It also involves carrying an image or appearance of a professional.

This is an invaluable ethic as it defines everything you do within the organization you work for. Your competence (as explained in another chapter) must be without question.

Talking about self-control, there will be situations (especially when dealing with clients or other co-workers) that an outburst in words may be likely to occur. Such outbursts could create more tension in the workplace and disrupt the workflow. It could also attract some measure of discipline as well.

In such situations, self-control comes in handy. Chew your word many times before you say them. Keep your hands to yourself as much as possible. Remain polite and calm even in the midst of the tension.

Rona Obrien couldn't have said it better when he said, "In your personal life there are situations where you will be angry, shout, start an argument or be difficult with other people. While you don't want to entirely remove your individual personality at work, you must be able to dampen down the negative sides"

Professionalism requires that you project positivity at all times.

The ethics explained in this chapter are by no means exhaustive. I have highlighted these ones to buttress the entire subject matter of this book.

Besides knowing these ethics, practice them. Incorporate them into your daily life right at the level you are now. The practice of these principles will not suddenly kick out of the blues when you attain a certain level or position in life.

Start now.

Start today.

Chapter Thirteen

How I Played in the World Cup

HOW I PLAYED IN THE WORLD CUP

A lesson on resting in God

The South Africa 2010 World Cup was notable for many reasons: it was a reminder that Africa had the potential to shape the globe, it revealed the united African voice that we've always clamored for.

Football may not be my favorite sport, but this one had an impact on me because I had the rare chance to attend one of the major games LIVE in the stadium. If for anything, I built up my football spirit and was good to go. But you know, life throws curve balls when you least expect. The big shots picked their best choice and edged most people out – including me. I stood no chance. Later on, the opportunity trickled down to the level I was, by some reason, I was edged out of it yet again.

Eventually, a week to the event, one of the employees that was selected had some challenges with one of the vital documents needed for the trip, so the slot became open.

"Would you like to have my slot?" the lady in question asked me politely. I was elated and affirmed my interest to be part of the trip.

However, the news travelled so fast that the Head of Department got wind of this development. That should not be a problem, but then, the head of department was somewhat disagreed that the woman offered her slot. It was supposed to remain open. The slot was taken away from me yet again. In that same time, a lady was offered the slot, but few days to travelling, her Visa was declined and then without any further argument, the slot was handed back to me.

This event reminds me of the Patriarch; Isaac, who went through contention over the wells his Father – Abraham – had dug. He was the only child of his parents and he had every right to lay claim to the wells his father had dug, but the people of the land where he dwelt wouldn't have that. For every well he unstopped, they contended with him. He had to relinquish his right over those wells each time the men raised a brow about it. He kept doing this until he dug the last one in Gerar and they could no longer strive with him over that. He called it Rehoboth. The word "Rehoboth" means Open space. Isaac said, "Now the Lord has made room for us, and we shall be fruitful in the land."

In many ways, this event points to our lives. As you navigate your path in life, there will be moments where it seems opportunities yanked from your hands. People and policies may appear as obstacles to your progress, in those moments, understand that the battle is the Lords and not yours.

In the face of opposition that you can do little against, trust God. Hold on to Him and to His promise tightly. He is too faithful to fail you. This has been the story of my unusual career journey. I have had opportunities yanked off but God has consistently made room for me.

In 2020 I started a house fellowship group I called Rehoboth, little wonder for God has indeed made room for me in his kingdom, in my career, in my life. Yes, I got the job in the Oil and Gas industry that I prayed about.

Against all odds, at a very senior position despite my being new in the industry. Yes I birthed my dream in the entertainment industry and started off my own production company on the side with a few productions already to my credit. Yes I continued my help mission by recruiting fresh people into my personal pay role as a give back.

Key Lessons

- There is a time to fight for what is yours, and there are times to let God handle it. Knowing the difference determines the results we see in our lives.

- When you hold on to God's promises for your life and career, all that is yours will come to you.

Quirky Thoughts

To my fellow dreamers...

I want to address my fellow dreamers; people who, perhaps, feel they are not yet where they want to be or "deserve" to be.

You know you could reach every last one of your goals and still find yourself unfulfilled at the finish line.

The true essence of life lies in the in-between. It is in the striving or the journey that your excellence is birthed and shared with the world.

It is in the setbacks that your strength of character is developed.

In the unfinished dream lies the burning pulse of life that keeps people striving.

It is only a spell of the mind and an artificial deception that you will find fulfillment in fame, fortune, wealth, power, etc.

Life is lived here in the distance you have to travel to your dreams.

This is where the true magic happens - that is life itself.

Welcome to LIFE.

If you are still on your journey, enjoy the ride.

CHAPTER FOURTEEN

LIFE UNUSUAL

The wind blows where it wishes, and you hear the sound of it, but cannot tell where it comes from and where it goes. So is everyone who is born of the spirit.

- Jesus Christ

s I write this, I am seated in my home office couched at my desk and reflecting on the memories of the past 2 decades in my life and career. It has become obvious to me, yet again, that our life's journey comes with unpredictable twists and turns, but what brings the highest fulfillment is the undying quest to make a meaning out of every phase we find ourselves in.

I believe very strongly that the trajectory of our lives are not predictable or cast in stone. If it were, life would be one boring movie played over and over again.

Certainly, no human possesses the mental bandwidth to comprehend all the scenes, events, and outcomes of our lives.

This is why I trust – and you should, your journey into the hands of the Lord who directs, controls, and re-orders our steps.

Read the subtitle of this chapter again. Do you see the verse of scripture?

Our lives should very much look like the wind. The wind is light and invisible, yet powerful enough to move things, bring coolness, and when heavy enough, it could uproot buildings and displace items hundreds of miles from its current location.

The wind is not fixed – it cannot be bottled in a jar or iced in the refrigerator. It is free-spirited and moves around unhindered and undeterred. This is the mindset you should have regarding your life. Don't be fixed like the mountains in the earth – change your thoughts constantly, challenge your beliefs and scale new heights. Like the wind, don't stay fixated on what is not working, do not hold on to hurts, grudges and disappointments. Move. At the heart of the unusual life is the desire to keep on moving while travelling light.

At the end of our lives and journey in whatever area of purposeful expression, we should be able to look back with the benefit of hindsight and see that we ended up a thousand times better and different than when we first started the journey.

The stories and events written in this book are factual and true. At the outset of my career, I had no inkling how the events would play out. While there were plans, hopes, and big dreams, I didn't see the whole journey.

Certainty is not ours to seek. The cross we are to carry is that of vision, a commitment to diligence and growth, and the pursuit of purpose in every place we find ourselves. This, inevitably, will bring each one of us to the expected end –that big place that we have been created for.

ABOUT THE AUTHOR

Winifred is a Lawyer and an experienced HR and Corporate Communications Professional with over 23 years' experience, largely in multinational environments in expatriate roles and also local capacity.

She holds a Bachelor's degree in Law, a Master's degree also in Law and an MSC in International Human Resource Management from Cranfield University, UK.

She is a member of the Nigerian Bar Association (NBA), Chartered Institute of Personnel Management of Nigeria (CIPMN) and a member of the learning and development faculty of the institute.

She is also an active member of the Society for Human Resources Management (SHRM) and currently serves on the Nigerian board of SHRM as Executive Director.

She is the founder and CEO of WinifredUnusual Productions; an outlet that reflects her passion for the creative industry.

Currently, she has several Productions to her credit, some of which have been entered for the most prestigious awards in the creative industry.

She loves to provoke thoughts in people and this led to the creation of a platform called Quirky Thoughts where she shares insightful nuggets to get her audience thinking in the right direction.

She believes that there can be multiple expressions of one person.

REFERENCES

- The 7 Habits of Highly Effective People, by Stephen Covey

- The Principles and Benefits of Change by Dr. Myles Munroe

- Lean in, Sheryl Sandberg

- Unwomen.org

- The Bible

www.ingramcontent.com/pod-product-compliance
Lightning Source LLC
Chambersburg PA
CBHW070518160726
48003CB00004B/1612